*Six W...*

If I were allowed just one word to describe Sarah Gordon's latest poetry collection, *Six White Horses*, I believe I would have to go with *smart*: She takes ostensibly familiar topics—love, death, religion, history—and cants them at new angles. Gordon summons in her own words the shadows of important well-known voices, among them Emily Dickinson ("A good aim can take / the top of the head / clean off"); Wallace Stevens ("inky tributaries / of deception"); and Jesus and Robert Frost in cahoots ("Over the stove, / burners caked in grease, / a sign, a line, a motto, / a reminder of wholeness,"/ holiness: Do unto /others, say, or two roads / diverged and all that."). If you give me another word or three, I'd have to consider *musical, dense, beautiful* and (in a positive way) *mean*. Ask me for a favorite title and I'd be torn amongst "On Memory, That Bitch," "The *Whens*," and "An Assortment of Astonishing Impersonations." Fortunate me, to be so torn.

—Stephen Corey, poet, essayist, and editor
emeritus of *The Georgia Review*

Sarah Gordon's *Six White Horses* is a poetic reminder that Memory is the mother of the Muses. Her poems offer poignant renderings of the people and particulars that belong to her own personal past and powerfully evoke those that haunt our own minds and hearts. Gordon's poems are vivid in their depiction of a lost time and place, rife with homely images that appeal to the eye and awaken in our consciousness the precious nature of everyday objects we take for granted—"sideboard, coal scuttle, fire screen, low boy"— reminding us of the extravagance of ordinary life. Gordon's poems tread sacred ground, even as they expand upon sanctity's terrain. Her imagined colloquies with celebrated saints, seers, and mystics, including Simone Weil, Dorothy Day, Thomas Merton, Flannery O'Connor, and the Pope, confess her own spiritual urgings, along with a wariness of conventional religion and its limitations as a means of access to truth. By turns witty and charming, wry and bittersweet, Gordon's poems bravely convey the late-in-life urgings of a nimble mind and a fierce spirit. Like salt in the full flush of its flavor, these are poems to be savored.

—Angela Alaimo O'Donnell, author of *Holy Land* and
*Andalusian Hours: Poems from the Porch
of Flannery O'Connor*

In Sarah Gordon's poem, "Plato Sounds a Note of Caution," Plato speaks of the various consequences of the written word, its all-encompassing power. Surely Gordon took him literally, for here in her most recent collection, *Six White Horses*, is the written word writ large. From memories of her mother decked out as a gypsy—the shock of it—to the heart-rending memorial to a friend, to her tribute to famous believers, her close examination of *The Book of Kells*, and the marvelous "Owls in Daylight" that opens with an eye-opening, honest appraisal of herself—always the power of language. How clear and precise the metaphors and her fierce attention to detail. I never knew that a pope wore scarlet shoes and that Cotton Mather's nose was pocked with blackheads. The things you learn in poetry!

—Alice Friman, author of *Blood Weather*

Sarah Gordon writes about "the lasso of language" in her first poem here, and after that, we're off and running, trying to get that rope around the world's neck, to haul it in and tame it. Fat chance! The task is impossible, but isn't it fun? Isn't it a joy to wonder where we'd be now if Adam and Eve hadn't eaten the apple, to hear our friend say *I can't get my head around that* and imagine what it'd be like if that head became plastic wrap pulled taut over mountain, prairie, highway? The last poem, too, touches on the diehard cowpoke work ethic that animates this whole collection, and it, too, is a beauty. But then so is every poem between.

—David Kirby, Robert O. Lawton Distinguished
Professor of English, Florida State University

# Six White Horses

## POEMS

## Sarah Gordon

MERCER UNIVERSITY PRESS
*Macon, Georgia*

MUP/ P712

29  28  27  26  25      5  4  3  2  1

Books published by Mercer University Press are printed on acid-free paper that
meets the requirements of the American National Standard for Information
Sciences—Permanence of Paper for Printed Library Materials.

Printed and bound in the United States.

This book is set in Adobe Garamond Pro.

Cover/jacket design by Burt&Burt.

Cover art used with permission of the artist:
"Six White Horses," acrylic on wood panel by Jeanie Tomanek

Library of Congress Cataloging-in-Publication Data

Names: Gordon, Sarah, 1941- author.
Title: Six white horses : poems / Sarah Gordon.
Other titles: Six white horses (Compilation)
Description: Macon, Georgia : Mercer University Press, 2025. |
Identifiers: LCCN 2024054764 | ISBN 9780881460452 (paperback)
Subjects: LCGFT: Poetry.
Classification: LCC PS3557.O686 S59 2025 | DDC 811/.54—dc23/eng/20241129
LC record available at https://lccn.loc.gov/2024054764

*This little book is dedicated to all of the strong, impassioned, and often ornery women I've known and loved.*

*Also by Sarah Gordon*

POETRY

*Distances*

*The Lost Thing*

LITERARY CRITICISM

*Flannery O'Connor, In Celebration of Genius* (Editor)

*Flannery O'Connor, The Obedient Imagination*

*Flannery O'Connor, A Literary Guide to Flannery O'Connor's Georgia*

# Contents

# Acknowledgments

"Hiding Again from the Jehovah's Witnesses," "Without," *Southern Poetry Review*;

"Crows," *Salt 5/6*;

"Catholic Colloquies," "Ambiguous Loss," "The Endless Undiluted Silence," "Nothing to Hold On To," "Substitute," *The Christian Century*;

"Catholic Colloquies" won The Excellence in Poetry Award, Best Church Press Awards, 2022

"Diagramming," *Miramar*;

"*Ach*, the Shadow of the Spinster," *The Georgia Review*;

"On *The Book of Kells*," "Sur l'existence éphémère," "Volute," *Christianity and Literature*;

"Point of Entry," *Salvation South;*

"Giving Up the Father," *Kestrel*

# The Old Adversary, Redrawn

*"The past is relieved of its feudal duties to the present, to us.*
*It can walk freely."*
Maria Stepanova, *In Memory of Memory*

# Nothing To Hold On To

When the lasso of language misses its mark,
falls limp in the dust, the horse gets away,
gallops triumphantly out of sight,
and there's nothing to connect the horse
to you, you to the horse,
nothing to hold on to

You see photos of those boys in India
who ride the tops of boxcars,
their bare feet pressing the steel,
an arm reflexively clutching the air
to steady the ballast that is the body

or that first ship way back when,
boldly sloshing away from the shore,
tethered only to the unfathomable deep

# The Fields Behind Us

*Memorial Day the First, 1865, Charleston, SC*

Always something
behind what we white
folks say, I confess.
Just over our shoulders,
shadows of meaning.
Centuries of behind
and before and shifts
in the saying,
maybe slight at first,
like small errors
in the ledger.

Cotton. Think about it.
Overplanted, planted over:
that furrow's plowed.
Always something behind
what they say, those
planters: mules, slaves,
lies across the page,
inky tributaries
of deception.

Tremulous fingers
pluck at the boll.
Reach, pull, release.
Reach and pull.
Figures in the field,
distant, bent, dark.
Children too. Raising
their eyes. Busy

in the heat. Industry.
Industrious. Dusty

those fields behind us.
We won't look, don't
have to. Work getting
done. Earth, sweat.
Come on inside. Sit.
We'll tell you what
it all means. Meant.
We'll write it down.
You can read it
for yourself.

# A Priori

What if, before she bit into it,
she handed the apple to him
but it fell and bumped
its perfect skin on the perfect
surface at their feet

What if then she'd bent
to pick it up just as he'd
leaned down and their heads
like two smooth eggs just
missed striking and cracking
wide open, white and yolk
all over the place

What if then they began
to giggle at the near
miss until they
could barely stand
upright (or were they
upright then?)
and soon they moseyed
off, leaving the apple,
and went about their
business being the first
in line first hands raised
in class first to feel
the moist and pleasing
ache (was there such
a thing as ache?)
of bodies together
and apart

And what if the apple,
pristine, lying there still
on the perfectly earthy
earth were only a distraction
(there were distractions
then) for the poet
who chanced upon it
and with it struck
and bruised the page

# Family Lines

When I left for school with a spot on my shirt
my mother said, *That won't be noticed
on a galloping horse.* My father, in the shower,
was singing *Shall we gather at the river*
and never heard me leave the house.

*That's enough to make a preacher
lay his Bible down,* Mother whispered,
leaning over the sink as she scrubbed
the pot with the frightening news: the Asian
War *With the cross of Jesus going on*

*before.* My brother was called,
not an especially Christian soldier,
and shortly afterward Daddy left
the church, provoked by peevish souls and petty
grievance, but mostly furious with the Almighty.

Melancholy set in, a quotidian darkness
we all felt, near and far, grown children
not grown, babies of the heart, anxious,
turning over glasses of tea at dinner,
scorching shirts with a hot iron.

Mother said she felt *like the dog's hind leg,*
splitting a silence so thick *you could cut
it with a knife.* Truth is, we couldn't say.
Tempers rose. My father had ceased
*leaning on the everlasting arms.*
Sweet Jesus.

# Une Petite Cri de Cœur

Oh God, perhaps our clothing is too
soft against our skin, the sheets too
cool: baby's blanket, baby flesh.
Fine woven cashmere, fruit
of the loom, of the womb,
precious, delicious, milky.
We'll stay here. Warm, safe,
in the midst of a million stories,
bound around us, and of our choosing,
alluring detours around those burning
foreheads, parching tongues.

We'll stay
where bodiless voices answer
us from across the room, where
tuneful alarms lead to colorful
screens that play games, fit
in a pocket, place us here
or guiltless at the scene
of the crime, tiny screens
that direct us, connect us,
collect small change.

# The Old Adversary, Redrawn

A preliminary sketch:
*Rattus rattus,* that large black one, brought the plague
from the steppes of Central Asia to the Crimea,
its stiff tail snapping in the hulls of ships
all the way to Europe and back again.
Meanwhile the *Pulex irritan*s, the flea
that beds in human flesh, covered congregants
in the Middle Ages, folks who thought bathing
bad for the health, those who, though prosperous,
were soon to be piled thick as sliced bread
in plague pits as far from town as the diggers
could dig them and the haulers haul
their pustulous remains.

Now that's one drawing.
Here's another: Instead of attending classes
in medical school, the young man slipped away into the woods
or just sat in the school parking lot for hours
until time to go home and play the intern
and family man at table
until he told one too many lies.
Because he said that, he had to say this.
Because he said this, he had to add that
and so on and so on.
Finally his lines were so tangled
he couldn't do a thing but find the pistol
and shoot wife, children, parents,
feeling all the while, of course, nothing.

Did you know that one rat's nest can become
in six months a colony of fifty?

That a male rat will continue to mate
with a female, even if she's dead?

Now, look over there:
The boys in the alley are burning
Styrofoam cartons and snorting up the fumes,
their lips raised from their gums like snarls.
Sufficiently pleased, they lie back in the trash,
they stretch their legs,
they kick each other and laugh.
Remember, if you see a rat,
it's weak, forced into the open
to look for food.

Finally, the family portrait:
We pull the blinds, turn on the light,
open our book to where we left off,
to where the path leads down to the river
and the day is endless and green.
For the moment, we forget
that even now the guards are seizing rats,
examining fleas, checking for the Black Death.
The fact is, rats exist in large numbers
where we do. They bite babies in the face,
consume cadavers and a third of the food supply.
Rats will not leave us alone.
Each morning when we wake,
we must once again sweep the floor,
press our ears to the walls.
We must reassemble the room,
knowing full well
we can never put everything back
where it belongs.

# Catalpa

When it's spring and the narrow-
winged sphinx moth has deposited
its larvae on the furry underside of
the catalpa's wide leaves,
when the shapeshifter eggs
stretch into the lovely black-velveted
caterpillar, that worm will turn,
consume its very birthplace, only to
be itself consumed by the fish
your father will catch in the river nearby;
that is, when the worms have done
their work, you have only to wait
until the seed pods darken,
as they will in October,
and you may cut and smoke
your first Indian cigar.
If you're tall enough,
you might pull down a limb,
if you're not, you climb,
perhaps skinning your legs
on the bark, used in olden days
as sedative or antiseptic,
now only the final obstacle
on your way to your desire.
Which is what, exactly?
Never mind. You snap off
a pod, taking care not to split
it, for it's full of papery seeds,
each with a dainty tuft of hair
on either end as though it had fancied
up for the occasion, your first time,
the first defiance of your mother,

who tells you what it will lead to,
as if more than your dress
will be soiled. Yet with her
sewing shears you'll snip the ends
of the pod, to make something
the tree never thought of,
your brother did, and he,
with his stolen matches,
his two-year head start,
will show you how to light.

# Lit

Perhaps Thoreau was first to say
live in the now, split the log
before you, look around
but not too far,
or you might glimpse Emerson
breathing frostily as he ransacks
the sky, or Walt lollygagging
down the path, loving everything,
until Eliot tells him no.
Don't listen for the train,
it's coming. So is the night.

Light the lamp, turn the page,
pick up where you left off:
the hero under Calypso's spell
tongues and nibbles the moment,
while part of him, the narrator
that is, has his eye on the door,
his feet on the floor, something
about him ready already
for the long journey home.

# Without

A while ago it was the shadow at the window,
the rustling you heard under the bed.

Now the wind presses in, unsettling the drapes.
In come fear and shivering, the cold air,

and with them the certainty you'll never
see her again, not on this earth.

In the stricken look of the ones
who receive your news, you see pity,

your own unbelief. You knock fiercely
on grief's door, seeking a word, afraid

to enter, unwilling to leave. The comforters
crowd around, winding the sheet.

The ritual unfolds as it must. Soon the line
breaks for you. You take your place.

The words of the faithful fall at your feet,
you step over and around them as others

before you have done. One giant step
forward. Two. Three. With. Without.

# Ancestry

The family crest over there
is dusty, been squatting on that
wall since our great aunt
died, she who hung it

in the first place. Great
Aunt Jule, big-boned and tall,
imposing, scared the devil
out of us children

when she toddled out of her
Model T (hat, gloves, and all)
and took her place at the table
to talk. She loved to talk.

Smacked her lips when
she began a story, as though
preparing to eat a full meal,
settling in for fried chicken

and biscuits. Never married,
but lusted for it, we thought,
sizing her up as The Old Maid
in the silly game of cards

we played when it rained.
No one wanted to be her!

If we could
stitch together those pieces
of her telling into a semblance
of order, a colorful, quilted

assortment of anecdote,
passion, gossip, and joke,
and toss out the scraps of
the mean, the mad,

and the outrageous,
maybe we could see more
clearly who the hell we are

# A Falling Out

From the corral of the family,
from the edge of the table

somebody's chair pulls
away, scraping the floor.

Somebody rises, places
her napkin on the table,

a wadded flower,
a signifier: a feverish,

impulsive departure.
Somebody else gasps.

Somebody vaguely
protests. Nobody moves.

It's a falling out. Not
a falling over or down,

but grave, for soon
after the garrulous host

had intoned his blessing,
the heart-wound happened,

the temperature rose,
her tether snapped loose.

*Food's getting cold,*
somebody says.

Forks rise. The platters
are passed, knives engaged.

Silence ensues,
and then

the weather,
the news.

# Crows

They know each other and know us.
Is that like God? They're on the front
lawn and perking around each other,
birdfellows, comrades of a certain era.
I like them, but I fear them,
with their ominous messages
from God knows where.
What I like is knowing
they're smart, companionable, as though
they're my soul friends, *anamchairde.*
They arrange funerals for those
whose sticky feathers and closed throats
they knew or remember. They talk
among themselves, in crowtalk, and
somehow they understand.

# Furnishings

Sideboard, coal scuttle,
fire screen, low-boy,
Queen Anne chair
with turned-up toes, fake
Queen Anne chair with oversized
turned-up toes, mahogany
dining table, your grandmother's
marble-top, baby grand
Steinway, red velvet sofa
(Duncan Phyfe), cane-bottom
rocking chair re-caned,
your father's wire rims,
his letters to your mother,
the Harvard Classics set
she purchased monthly
for a year, tiny vial of Patou's *Joy*
you bought for her in Geneva in '68
(unopened in a dresser drawer);
the mounted deer head overseeing
the den, brown marble-eyed,
(your father the proud hunter);
Roy Rogers record player for 45
records (Fats Domino, Elvis,
Sam Cook, The Platters),
yellowing stacks of *Look* and *Life,*
vinyl dinette set, empty Dutch
ceramic cookie jar, six bloated
Green Stamp books, your father's
roomy leather chair (*his* chair),
the first and only dishwasher, a child's
cash register with a drawer that opens,
your dusty diary, eternally incomplete,

scrapbooks scattering their contents
on the closet floor, faded polaroid
snapshots

Only a fraction of the heart's inventory,
the glossary of its moments, without the views
and soundscapes of faltering mortal attendance—
the long view to the barn out the kitchen window,
the cool tiles beneath your bare feet on the den
floor, the beveled glass in the front door before
which your life came and went, the maid's
own bathroom (off limits to you), the dog's
insistent bark at the back porch door,
your brother fuming over Latin verbs,
the sound of his textbook as it hit the wall,
your mother's steps on the stairs
as she sought you out to tell you,
to tell you what she shouldn't have
but did anyway,

for which you must forgive her
her secrets, her pain

# The Endless Undiluted Silence

I wish I could reach you there,
where it is you live now, the ripples

of days cascading to no sound, where
it is you aren't. I can't get beyond that wall,

I can't find you anywhere. Not in the nightly

news, not on the patio near the birdfeeders

where the chickadee and charming ladderback
tremulously light. I can't find you. You can't hear

me when I point them out, our elusive visitors.
You are patient with me, with my strident

resolve to show you the birds, the fleeting
evening light as it sifts through the trees.

And suddenly I am desolate, outraged.
I want to protest, to berate, even damn

this mortal ripening, the path that brings
us close to joy, but no closer.

# The Happiness Quotient

*-If the shoe fits…*

Look! Life is one lilting, breathtaking up-
swing after another of the hammock,

one stirring vermilion sunset after another
dutifully snapped and captured,

another fine meal with dearest friends
assuring confidence in life's satiety.

Your pulse races, you weep happily,
gratefully on the voyage out,

as the ship bumps from the hold,
the sea the bed you'll sleep on;

you think, tamed. Istanbul at dawn,
minarets tipping gold. You recite a poem.

You're in the taxi into Berlin: the city
still divided but comfortable, neither alien

nor frightening after all, history's vagaries
notwithstanding. Here you are on the edge

of it. History, that is. On the safari you find
that the clothes you chose are just right;

you fit into the scene, the last piece of the puzzle,
and the gazelles leap solely for your pleasure.

Look! Let's have only the prettiest, please.

# Dead People Talking

When you lie still in your bed at night
and the wind has mysteriously abated,
stretch your legs on the cool unsullied
sheets, and wait for the sounds of home
to subside—the spitting icemaker emptied,
the squirrels static in the attic, time stacked
in cans and boxes in the pantry—
listen.

They're talking. If not to you, to each other
and the dead before and around them,
beyond the crepe and the vault, even
beyond the pyre and the urn. Lean close,
don't move a muscle. Don't even swallow.
How good is your hearing? How well
do you listen? Can you? You know
you want to know.

Sibilants and fricatives and some caesuras, too,
adhere like Velcro to each other, just now,
in this moment, sounds close to words,
parsed out in lines you can stretch across
a page, and then down and back. Pull them out
and stand them up in your inky scrawl, or set
them in type. Say them aloud. Repeat.
*Attendez.*

# Ambiguous Loss *

*(term given by psychiatrists to describe the emotional state of those
who do not know whether their lost loved ones are dead or alive—
The New Yorker, Jan 16, 2023)*

For starters, the missing cat.
Soon enough, high school pals,
college boyfriends, harmless
rivals, that beloved professor
you thought you'd never forget,
glasses strung on a cord around
her neck, that imposing gaze.
The world stretches out, pulled
taut, investigated, penetrated,
pummeled, and parched,
and you're forced to behold,
beyond the back yard
and distant border, unsettling
images of hordes foraging
for food in the desert, bending
over the burning earth in desperate
prayerful attendance. You must
witness, as well, the young mothers,
babies strapped to their backs,
some treading water, others
sliding down muddy banks.
Seeking asylum, they're briefly
tented and tended by others—
kinsmen, natives, even a few traders—
before moving toward that boundless
wall. The wall is real, of course.
Beyond it is what we cannot know.
Or know what finally happened to:

cousins, allies, colleagues, multitudes
of distraught strangers seeking
kith and kin. Forensics forever
beats its head against that cold concrete,
searching for DNA, examining the fragile
toys strewn about the scrapyards of our lives,
riffling through stacks of inventory,
always encountering, oh yes indeed,
a stunning halt to retrieval.

# If Love Leaves Your Life

The lone piper turns his back
and wends his way beyond the hill.
The few remaining listeners
scatter, a congregation now lost
to the inevitable end of things,
as the mournful tune fades,
the sun sets.

If love leaves and leaves for good,
not much chance of saying more,
of wishing *before* were here again.
All this is truth, you know it well.
Nobody need say what a joyless
path you're walking, what trackless
steps you take.

If love leaves and locks the door
and goes in hiding far away,
there'll be no map, no treasure
hunt, no time to reconnoiter.
Only this: some shredded
tissue, a bitter note, perhaps
a filibuster: the tale you'll have to tell.

# The Stain

Long into the night
we held the stain
up to the light
and turned it
turned it turned it
round to annunciate
its truth.

Purple-edged, maybe
blue, the stain
seemed of such
a hue as to bewilder,
even alarm
those of us who'd
come to question

why it could not
be removed, as it
surely behooved
our science to do—
and quickly, too.
Staring at it did
no good, no good

at all. Where
to put it, how to shut
it out, bury it deep,
we asked ourselves.
It was electric,
a convoluted
dialectic we couldn't

enter or ascertain
as plain fact or
put in words, how
to abrogate, elucidate,
except perhaps to say
aloud: Behold
the bloody mystery!

# Antics

How strange or odd some'er I bear myself,
As I perchance hereafter shall think meet,
To put an antic disposition on.
Shakespeare, *Hamlet*

# An Assortment of Astonishing Impersonations

1

When I was a child, mid-century last,
every year the white men of certain
standing held a minstrel show,

dressing up in black suits or even
tuxedos, creating a decided funereal
look, and smudged their faces so black

their pink lips looked painted, large.
Before the show they posed, smiling
widely into their mirrors, turning

this way and that, offering their wives
the chance to be kissed, or *bussed*
(as that intimacy was often called),

to partake of their charcoaled darkness,
the ladies feigning horror at this crossing
of the line, the violation of taboo.

The auditorium filled fast,
three tiers of rising bleachers creaking
with the nervous weight of that semicircle

of white eyeballs, the grinniest grins
you ever saw. Yet, to my dismay, my father,
the interlocutor, remained serious and white.

He was the straight man, the instigator,
his job to elicit from those simpleminded

darkies, Brudder Tambo, Brudder Bones
and Zip Coon, their foolishness,

to the boundless glee of the audience.

And Jim says to Huck, "Yit dey say Sollermun
de wises' man dat ever live. . . .
But whut use is half a chile?"

2

At Halloween, after school, the fair assembled
on the playground. Face-painting was not then
a thing, though mothers in costumes offered

their wares. We were all white mid-schoolers,
learning the continents, multiply-and-divide,
and separating subjects, verbs, and modifiers

on clean, confident lines across the page.
How odd and how amusing, then, to find
my own mother a scarved and bejeweled gypsy

behind the white sheet of the fishing booth!
We were to select a rod, nothing more than
the small branch of a tree with a string

on its end, and with great expectation, fling
it over the sea of the sheet and pull in what
we caught.  We held our collective breath.

But somehow the catch—a small plastic doll,
a crayon, or an eraser—was never to match
the glamour of my mother's overpainted

lips, her golden hoop earrings, long full skirt,
and that bolero blouse, low-cut, almost
revealing her cleavage, her untamed

beauty, and another life altogether.

3

So what if a poet decides to get in the head
of another poet who's dead and presume

to live her quotidian life, even as she'd read
the paper in a comfortless rocker on the porch

or prayed in the local church, stared at
the bloody sunset, or gossiped with friends,

and then tell it all in a voice that could be
hers?  Or what if a poet places on purpose

the passionate letters of his ex-, verbatim,
in a poem and says it's so and defies friends

and others who urge him not to, who warn
him of theft and bad taste and distorting

her and their distressing, tempestuous life
together? What if the poet places his own mother

in his poem, with her pursed lips and prejudice,
and what if we come to believe him and hate her?

What if the interlocutor and the gypsy exist only
on these pages as this poet contrives them?

Just consider someone with designs on your life,
someone creating in you the style of the day,

clothing your thoughts, tucking in and letting
out the wardrobe of your being with what

that someone wants or needs for you to wear—
and with only the paltriest fabric, most careless

stitches, the tailor's capricious whim:
Astonishing impersonation indeed!

# Bites

When the daughter was ten, she was chased
by a dog and then it was her father taught her
always to greet a strange one with palm out
so that she could be sniffed and certified.

Lesson learned, she tried to follow it
for the rest of her life, the open hand
to strangers, in the hope never to be bitten or,
for that matter, to bite, offering the most

prudent of meetings and greetings. All of life
would work this way, or so she believed:
missteps avoided, accidents elsewhere,
though she must be vigilant, she knew.

She was careful to swat away the mosquito
headed directly into her face, to watch
for snakes in tall grass, to consider how
others saw her, to smile into the mirror.

Thus she was surprised when the wasp,
nestled in the hem of her skirt, stung
hard. She heard the velocity of her screams
burning the walls of the house, in the fear

and promise of all wounds to come.
Later, of course, she learned to use
that voice to set her world straight,
and when she became strident, straight

didn't matter so much. Shouting
did. In what seemed a primordial rage
she screamed out as though she were
an impersonator, but mostly somebody

she couldn't recognize, invective spilling
out all over the floor, into the hall, staining
the carpet, blooding her eyes, and burning
her cheeks. She bit her tongue mightily.

# The *Whens*

When the deaths reach ten thousand,
we tuck in our weapons, we cease to shout.
When the water evaporates, the empty cistern
cracks in the heat, a sudden cleavage,
dry from dry, leaving nowhere
to catch the rain, nowhere.

When the grass begins to green,
we gather the lambs and look them
in the eye, marking one of them
for the altar. When the talk stops,
we know it's twenty before or twenty after.
When we decide to nap, the noise

begins, an atonal arhythmic banging
that turns out to be inside the house,
inside the body, nothing we can
sing to or scan, frightening us
maybe to death. When the power
fails, we light a lantern

or just sit in the dark, the heart's
cupboard bare, the clock stopped
or just pretending to stop
forcing us to sit still, to listen.
When the little snake dies,
we toss its limp length

into the woods or bury it
and say we're sorry for its role
in the drama, which, some time ago,
we wrote. When the lovemaking ends,

we pretend to sleep, instead considering
all that did and did not happen.

When we find what we are looking for,
we hold it. After a while we relax
our grip. We cannot explain how it is
that when the guest arrives,
all the joy runs out of the bowl
lickety-split, how it is

that hunger vanishes when
we are sick with love and returns
after we say the vows, fracturing
the food supply, leaving nothing to share.
We cannot explain. When words fail,
we flail our arms like the shipwrecked,

leaping and dancing the calisthenics
of rescue to sky and sea, cartoon
figures desperate to be saved
or understood. When the planes
pass overhead, we pick up our rifles,
sighting the threat in the crosshairs,
glancing at one another to see
who'll be first to pull the trigger.

Like swarms of gnats, the *when*s
encircle us, fly into our eyes,
our open mouths. We wince
and spit, we seek cover, to hide away
in some place of plain and simple
utterance, a cave, a trench, a when-
less, unstrung land without contingent,
or history, with no before at all.

# Fixed Points

Who fixed the fixed point,
I'd like to know,
who thumbtacked the spot
to steer us through our drunken
roiling? Who righted the room,
returning the lamps to their proper
position, showing us the door?

.

Your spilled drink is runaway
ink that spreads to the edge
of the page and drops
down onto your shoes,
stippling them with a small
pointillist painting that will surely
give you away

.

In Africa a certain figure,
robed and shoeless, silhouetted
by the sun, stands motionless
as the grave, watches the road,
and feels the hot wind rise
against this house
that is your body, mine

•

A black bud opens on your back
where you can't see it,
though you soon learn
that, even on the dry land
of your flesh, this lotus
in its stillness is rooting
in the shallows

•

Who was it, so sure we'd fight,
so certain of the outcome,
he made a place for us
to cool off, languish
in each other's presence,
wringing our idle hands,
nothing but mischief on our minds?

# Rock

When you hit your head on it,
knock somebody's brains out with it,
aim it at somebody's window,
or lean on it for your salvation,

perhaps it has become a poem:
It bursts the glass, opens the head,
rearranging reality and redefining
comfort. That ornery Peter

was called a rock, became It
and the Church, so we're told.
He never resembled a rock
to his friends, maybe only

later. That's metaphor, I guess,
part of what makes the rock
the rock and compelling.
It accrues interest.

Old Cotton Mather
got the real thing through
his study window for standing
up for the pox vaccine

way back then. What do
we mean when we say
hard as a rock except
to say nothing but a rock

can break it, if anything can?
Cleft, battered, smashed.
A shiver down the spine,
A tightening of the throat.

A good aim can take
the top of the head
clean off.

## Catholic Colloquies

1

# I invite Simone Weil to dinner

and though she has a big heart,
she has little appetite. I've set
the bread and wine before her
and bowed my head as though
in prayer. She's bent, but unbowed,
and stares into me through those
scary little round glasses, and I'm
exposed, defensive as a bird
in the crosshairs. Her bobbed
hair, pale face remind me
of someone I once knew, before
the war, someone who toiled
in the auto plant, someone who
really didn't belong there. That
girl was awkward, intense, finally
ill. Had to be taken away. Not
a worker, maybe a student.
Always in black, an angular figure
flinging off her cape, stepping
up to the assembly line as if
she were one of us. Now, she sits
before me. Something about her
eyes, hard but kind, summons
me to a strange extravagance,
to the fulfilling final gesture,
for a moment reminding me
of something I wish I had.

2

# I'm serving up soup with Dorothy Day

Honest to God, I've nothing to say,
as I stand by her reproachful, skinny
frame. We all know the resolve
in that square jaw. Her hands
are busy, see, strands of her hair refuse
to stay put, sliding out of that unkempt bun.
She serves bowl after bowl, efficient, cool
in her shapeless shirtwaist, washed nearly
to death. I hear she's some kind of saint,
someone who knows well what she's about—
after her long, lonely coming of age,
the birth of a child, the marches, the fasts,
the Berrigan boys—but I find her thorny,
almost cross. This woman's a warrior.
To the unbroken line of the poor and hungry,
she's matter-of-fact, magnanimously discreet,
charmless, not harmless: a white-hot wire.

**3**

# I joke with Flannery O'Connor about the Trinity

as we cross the field to the fence.
Two's company, three's a crowd,
I crow. Triangle? Equilateral?
And the Holy Spirit? Is that like
putting a Bounce sheet in the dryer
capturing all the electricity?

She's wearing that wide-brimmed
straw hat, frayed, keeping her face
safe from the sun. Saving face,
I think wickedly. Still, she's
patient with my foolishness.

I hear myself gracelessly posing
my questions, saying something
one way and then another, as though
trying on a glove of one size, then
reaching for something looser, with
more give, as she bumps along on
the aluminum crutches, likely savoring
our distance from the house. I want
to say Watch the ditch, May I help,
but my words are trapped in my fear
for her, my fear of her damned
sufficiency, complete, entire.

4

## I seek an audience with the Pope

Not the old one with the scarlet shoes!
The new-old one of the falling face,
generous grin, he who's always cloaked
in Cloroxed white, like a large fresh cloud
over us. He carries his own bags upstairs,
clump, clump, slowly, methodically,
his scuffed oxfords run down at the heels.
An audience, you say? *Audire, audientia:*
I will be the small soul before him,
with all my questions queued up,
bumping into each other like thirsty
children at the water fountain.
Kindly—he seems kindly, and won't
take his eyes off me as I climb down
from this tree, scraping my knee,
calling to him, *Father, Father.*

5

# I am slow dancing with Thomas Merton

before he was Father Louis, before
that staired mountain, before his lovely vision
on the street in Louisville. He's not quite bald
yet, nor quite Catholic. We talk about France,
the sun on the trees in Provence, books.

Mostly, though, we talk about searching
and not finding, still thinking we'll see a sign,
our own path, God maybe. We confess
our guilt as bystanders in the renewal
of the world. But we're still young! we say.

Our hands sweat as we bump around
the floor, and I fall a little bit over his feet
and a little bit in love. The band is playing
a Piaf song, and some poor girl hovers over
the mic and tries to sing, a poor breathy
imitation, *Non, je ne regrette rien.*

# Diagramming

On a straight line,
as we're wont to measure time,
subject and verb

are first to be fixed:
named, separated like prattling
children sitting too close.

Modifiers swing out from
the base, adorn the branch,
add flesh to the bone.

Then the line that is time
and a sentence as well
extends seriatim into

the years, into that vastness
as into the sea, there
to slacken and tangle,

eternally twined.
There, too, tides of particles,
unseemly articles, wash ashore

only vaguely resembling
what once was good form:
the straightforward declarative,

guileless and clear,
stretching out on the page
just the way our ripe bodies

first opened to love—eagerly
plotted, parsed,
and known.

# Fluidity

The word has resonance
and cachet these days.
I like to say it. I like to think it.
I'm not sure I want to be it.
Some like it there, in that
in-between space, maybe
like two people trying to sit
in one chair, or a river
losing its name as it flows
into the sea, then renamed,
its past only a veined tracery
on the map. If you squint
it's not there. *Fluidity*.

# Antics

I wonder who told the first joke,
got the first big laugh, who knew
what a laugh even was and how
to take it. Was it contagious,
a poke in the ribs of the next man,
and so on around the fire:
*Get it?   Get it?   Do you get it?*

Who decides what is amusing,
silly, or downright hilarious, who
sets the tone. Who was the first
to use a joke to begin a sermon,
to win some votes and be the center
of everything, at least for a while.

Who the first to use a laugh to shame,
to bully, to win first place in the line.
Who knew how to arouse a crowd,
to circle a pariah only to say at last,
*I was only joking   just being silly*
*Playing   meant nothing   no offense*

Who invented irony, the inside joke,
the secret verbal handshake for those
in the know—*oh you know!*—turning
laughter on its head, coins falling
from its pockets, clunkety clunk
clunk on the floor. A sad spectacle.

Who was the prophet, that wrinkled
old sod, who came on when summoned,
though crotchety, reluctant to speak,

who nonetheless caused the smug
to smile, the ravenous chorus to grasp
the king's crimes long before
the king himself had a clue

# Answers

"the whining in the rigging" Eliot, *The Dry Salvages*

In third grade I learned
to wrap my left arm around
my answers on the test.
I'd seen others do that,
hunching over their desks,
as if guarding treasure.
Who was so sure then,
I wonder, that their results
were the right ones?

                *

That same year
we began passing notes
up and down the aisles,
tiny, folded paper scraps
printed with life-changing
queries: I love you.
Do you love me? Check
the box, yes or no.
We hid those sweaty
missives to open up
later, when, alone,
we'd behold our bold
moves, aghast, pleased.

                *

Old Miss Lackey gave us
those pink catechisms
in Sunday School,
demanded we learn

the answers:
*Who made you?*
*It is God who has made*
*us and not we ourselves.*
The Ten Commandments.
Long before we knew
the facts of life, we could say
*jealous, covet, adultery.*

\*

The math text printed
the answers by chapter
at the back of the book.
We just had to know how
to get there: prove theorem,
solve equation. Remember
what you know. Take the next
step, the next. Call this trial
and error, but find
a predictable path.
Place your calculus
on the page.

\*

On the court, serve,
volley. Play the net,
but watch the back
line. A ball out is out.
Maybe some leeway
in the let serve, but,
no, not much. Might

be a love game.
Breathless.
Game, set, match.
Final.

\*

The windows barely open,
only the smell of the tea olive
sifts through. What would
happen if we raised the sash,
threw open the door,
let ourselves hear
*the whining in the rigging,*
and stepped out into
that furious wind,
mapless, and got blown
all over the place,
in fact—to smithereens?

## *Ach!* The Shadow of the Spinster

God! It's a body cast, permanent, an unbreakable chrysalis,
inescapable. It's the damned Old Maid card on the floor of the attic,
it's withered organs, shatterproof glass, it's words we can't use,
like *orgasm, ass.* It's a dead-end street, ye olde unplowed field,
all burnt-out summer, no fucking yield, no perpendiculars drawn
on the family tree, no lines at all. *That old lady smell,*
the nephews intone, scratching their privates, biding their time,
watching their watches or fondling a phone. It's progeny, privilege,
the secret handshake, she can't have *no* children, she just simply can't.
She's a doorstop, a spinster, a sister, an aunt. She's a *trillium erectum*
pressed dead and flat in The Book that still marks our couplings,
our deaths, the past in our midst as rank as her breath
when she flatlines, incinerates into ashy white death.
She's impeccably pure, released into history, or not.

# Proximities

When the yellowjacket removed his coat,
we were all a bit embarrassed for him,
for he was a scrawny one, looked to be

a fat gnat, unless you looked closely,
and we did. We always do.
Then did you notice

the drooping eyelid of the priest
when he laid the wafer in your palm,
saying the holy words only

to you, as he moved among
the communicants, his stole
wine-spotted, uneven,

down on one side
more than the other, so much
that we worried he might lose it

to the floor, which, you note,
needs a good sweep and polish,
certainly before the wedding

next week, when we'll all gather,
and from our sly peripheral vision
take note, on the lookout
for sagging neckline, fading cheek,

the old animosity, in proximity,
scarcely able to conceal itself,
though lotioned, perfumed
and freshly combed.

# How To Know If Your Heart Is Strong

They say to press the nails of your index
fingers together, and if a diamond of light
appears, your heart is strong.

Now stretch your hands, spread
your fingers wide, feel that distance,
the fissure of detachment.

Touch your face, slide your forefinger
over your lips, down to chin, around
your jaw to the soft strange

lobe of the ear. Grasp the lobe
with finger and thumb until
you know where you are.

Rest. With thumb and finger
encircle an eye, left or right.
Squint the other eye tight

to make your own camera obscura.
Look carefully at what the light
encloses. Try not to blink.

Feast on the intimacy of shape
and color, propitious, free.
This is a love poem, right now
right here in front of you.

# Hiding Again from the Jehovah's Witnesses

Testimonials cower me, especially
of the spirit. I don't want to open my door
to earnest strangers, I don't want to meet
their eyes. Their cheerful chatter
on the other side of the screen
assumes an intimacy I do not feel.
They dress for Sunday on Saturday
and open their Bibles, the leather cracked,
finger a verse or two, and they're certain.
So now I hover beside the windowless
wall in the front hall, where I hear,
in the domestic distance, the washer
sloshing, the dryer spinning my clothes
in and out of control, and perhaps
the swish of angel wings. My intrepid
visitors ring twice, quietly awaiting
this reluctant soul, thrice-baptized,
loved beyond measure, or so
I've been told. But I don't want
to hear news of the end (it's coming,
you know), I won't learn the signs
to watch for: rivers shriveling here,
sandbagged there, polar bears
in our back yard, birds plummeting
from the sky through no fault of their own,
and worse, the buzzing ears and frantic
hearts that lead us to run, lickety-split,
through red lights, guard-rails, and
family fortunes, with an occasional
backward glance, the pillar of salt be damned.
The witnesses from Jehovah want in,
they want me to be watchful. They say

that's what Jesus wants.
But I am leaning low and still
on the other side of the wall,
and when I close my eyes,
I'm invisible.

# My Grandmother Was a Thousand Years Old

My grandmother was a thousand years old
My grandmother was a hundred years old
My grandmother was old

After church on Sunday, we lined up
in her parlor to kiss her on the mouth,
a peculiarly intimate ritual, essential,

almost sacred. She was small in her chair,
sitting beneath an afghan the color of her lips.
She tipped her head up each time, mouth

puckered, expectant. I don't remember
her calling our names. We were many, though,
mostly children, and, God knows, she'd birthed eight.

How could she tell the seven girls apart?
The son, of course, stood by her rocker,
her sentinel and protector. He was my father,

the male heir for whom she'd waited long.
She clung to him for breath and life: her boy.
My mother, quietly repelled, stepped out of line.

But, for us children, kissing Grandmother's lips
was like sliding in to home plate, achieving
some kind of anointed state, accepted, confirmed.

# Cotton Mather's Melancholy

arrived when he least expected,
after his third wife, possessed
for years by the Devil, died
far beyond the realm of reason.

The preacher's lips dried out,
his tongue curled back against
his palate. Never a comely man,
he avoided the mirror,

yet when the glass caught him,
he saw his face, walrus-
like, sliding down onto
his neck, his ears so pulpy

that without the wig
they seemed not ears at all
just fleshy tubers fit
for planting. The pores

on his nose were black,
wanting years of scrubbing.
Not so his soul, he believed,
long convicted and cleansed.

How could anyone ever love
this face, he marveled, except
the Lord? And he whom
the Lord loveth oh yes certainly

But where exactly lies the Lord's
will, he muttered, remembering
that *rampant hag* and the others
drawn up and dropped gracelessly

from the gallows, a sanctified
drapery for all to see.
Innuendo, sibilant suspicion,
the mark on the body, the raising

of the brow. What's hallowed may not
be so. What's not is fretful and strange,
as loose as the river flooding its banks
lapping the path of the quotidian.
*Who was Cotton Mather?*
the schoolboy now asks.
*The man who rode horseback and hung
witches.* A mirthless man

god-fearing, hell-bent,
he yanks on the reins,
riding us, guiding us,
the bit as tight as a well-

wrought sermon, digging
into our jaw, drawing blood.
Don't hold on so tight,
we plead. Ease up, relax.

But the saddle is strictly
cinched, its leather groaning
beneath this portly spectral rider
who knows us and turns us
ever so slightly—and then

quite suddenly—off the lovely
road, into the vexing, judgmental,
and boundless dark

# Head Games

Talking in the new way,
you say, *I can't get my head*
*around that*, and I tease you:
your head is plastic wrap
pulled taut over mountain, prairie
and highway clear into the city,
swathing rooftop and tower,
the scratchiest of trees
the way Christophe wrapped
the Kremlin. Then to be helpful
I say, think of an equation
spread in small symbols across
a classroom board, filling it
entirely, and your mind supple
enough to turn all those corners
and cross the streets but
still not quite making it
to our front door.

Once, way back then,
you and I swore that if ever
we were blinded or knocked
senseless, we'd know
the smell of the other's
sweet flesh anywhere,
trusting entirely our
ravening appetite
and hyperbole's broad
brush.

Three cheers anyway
for memory's steamy
window and the fine
extravagance of feeling
that takes the wheel
and turns up the high beams!
Hurray for holding still
long enough
to get the shoes tied,
the collar straight,
to make the messy bed.

# Giving Up the Father

As in yielding, as in waving
the white flag of surrender,
meeting in the middle of
the field, handing him

over. As in giving up on
his swagger, his interruption
of everything in his big boots
and long list of orders.

Giving up the father,
as in replacing history with
a new kind of *tabula rasa*,
receptive to color and design.

As in turning the back
on the insatiable wish to please,
the labored laughter, the pose
and the poise to get it right

in the father's eyes. As in
knowing the secret handshake,
the pleasing invocation, and,
of course, the creed.

# Six White Horses

"I meant to write about death, but life came breaking in as usual."
Virginia Woolf, *Diary*

# On Memory, That Bitch

What a tiresome old player!
She winds her skirts around
her legs, she pulls her jacket
tight. She doles out shapes
from the past cavalierly,
never looking us squarely
in the eye. We finger an edge
or two of that old puzzle
we've been working most
of our lives, unfinished.
We've spread it piecemeal
on the table, noting the tangled
family line, the missing photos
in the album, our father's dark
betrayal, the words we heard him say.
Memory lowers her gaze in disdain:
she will ever remain vexatious,
powerful, the unreliable narrator
who tosses the long-lost pieces
willy-nilly on the dining room floor.

# The Goldfinch

When I lie down to sleep,
the overhead fan circling
madly, I think I hear a man
on a radio, (though I don't
own a radio) far away, grave,
all the news about a war.
His words sink and rise,
catapulting from there to
here on currents of dissonance,
from strangled battlefields,
broken borders, explosion.
Now, in my mind's eye and every-
where else, I see head wounds
soaking through their dressing,
limbs lost, a child or children,
numbed, reeling beneath
desolate birds of prey.
I see banks of countless bodies,
swathed in rotten clothing,
twisted as in a washer,
to be dried, sorted, put away.
Put away because they can't
get away or couldn't. Caught
in place, like that bird Fabritius
painted, its one leg tethered
forever to the perch by a single
silver chain that's hardly visible:
*The Goldfinch*, still, abiding.

# From the Land of Names

The moon complained
that the night moved too close,
was too familiar, flinging
at her from all sides
a dark and suffocating mantle.
When morning came, I broke
the news: just as I had told
the cat the night before
he has whiskers on his face,
I told the squirrel
he is called a squirrel
and has been for a while.
He said he didn't like
the sound of it.
We laughed together
about the folly of naming,
pathetic fallacies, the urge
to swing upside down
on the feeder
with some panache,
as though we're in control.
He flicked his electric tail
teasing me in clucks and shrieks,
squirrel-talk, a tongue,
he said, I didn't know.

At noon the red fox
halted in the drive,
looked me in the eye,
admonishing, *Please!*
We all have stories
of fleeing the woods
we know so well

and heading into the open,
of being seen and known
and named, our ornery
bodies bright with the light
of lunacy and exposed,
heading God knows where.
We've all been slapped
with nominatives
not of our own invention.

But, don't you know,
the moon said, when we stand
in the clearing, we always
look over our shoulders
back to the wood,
back to the tangle of memory,
to bird rests and beehives,
solitary blooms, back
to the first place.
There, the shaman
speaks to the honeybee
in honeybee-speak
and waits for a response.
There, our days begin
after delicious midday slumber,
when, in the silence
of glad awakening,
all is understood.
Nothing need be said,
No throat need be cleared
No thought need be taken,
for nothing can be diminished
nor changed nor embellished
by the urgency of utterance
the circumscription of word
the forfeiture of time.

# How It All Turned Out

*-in memory of Lucy Underwood*

You'll want to know everything,
of course, and I'll have time to tell you:

how you were sick for years
sicker and sicker, how your flesh

slipped away, your head fell.
Finally, your beloved piano,

your parents' sensible gift,
your collaborator, your accomplice,

your consort, became a burden,
a cumbrous legacy, a donation, a tax

break for somebody, ivory and mahogany
adding up your life, a cash register.

How family disappeared, many friends, too,
how some new ones came, doing your nails

and rubbing your legs now wasted
like the atrophied limbs of polio or rickets,

diseases pictured in our schoolbooks
but not the one that grabbed onto you,

tremored your hands and halted
your step. This is what I'll tell you

too, how one day when my own heart
began to believe it could bear no more

when you no longer talked but suddenly
lurched forward as though taking your leave,

I took your arm, held you still,
leaned in to catch your eye

and from somewhere way inside yourself
you smiled, a strangely effortless,

tender smile meant just for me,
all love, all love abiding.

*Sur l'existence éphèmère*

Mr. Ghosh stopped to water the geranium
before he began his descent from the 74$^{th}$ floor
and made it, bloodied, dusted, out the door
onto the street before the Tower fell.

Ghosh lived to tell the tale. My mother
wafting in and out of breath, dying, fretted
that her needlework was unfinished, roused
briefly to announce who best could stitch it

in her absence. Not just anybody, but the friend
with the steadiest hand. Our aged cousin, stroke-
stricken, rolled himself into the sunset every day
until the last, his chalky pastels on his lap.

What powerful impulse in the face of the end,
of nearly certain annihilation, the stairway filled
with smoke, seizes us? *La force de la vie?*
*L'élan vitale?* What curious instinct leads us

to wash up, put away the silver, spread the bed,
scratch an image, if not to edit our lives one last time,
put the finishing touch or flourish on the strangeness
and wonder of our story, *l'existence éphèmère.*

# How Things Work

Before I die, I'd like to know
more about how things work.
I'm embarrassed by what
I don't understand,
I have to say.
In fact, why I say
*I have to say,*
as though a gun
were held to my head,
I don't understand.
Besides that, all things
electric, digital,
or otherwise hooked up,
like our myopic
and bumbling friends
who stumble into
each other, marry
for love and are happy.
I'd like to understand
that, too. O, I confess,
my ignorance is vast.
Outside the house
I'm even shakier:
what goes on under
the hoods of automobiles,
how satellites bounce
the vulgar image
that always catches
somebody's eye,
how the ragged ozone
might be patched,
and just who

tore that cover
in the first place.
How does it happen
that the lovers I took
one by one
come to be friends
whose bodies no longer
bear my marks
but are eerily familiar,
like another version
of my own?
For that matter,
whatever happened to desire,
that blanket we lay under
in late afternoon,
or sometimes lay *on*
and played on
until we were played
out and at peace?
Where does that urgency
now hide, or has it
left the building
entirely, like Elvis,
who endures only
in sideburned impersonators
gyrating at state fairs?

# Volute

The fiddlehead fern
spooling out at close range,
loosening and stretching,

the spindle-shell, a gastropod,
out of sight, tucked in its spiral,
its wide lip open.

The imperceptible carving
on the bow of the ship,
the scrolled neck of the violin.

The loop of the bypass
round and round the city,
imperfect circles closing in.

The dancers' skirts full
and falling, tantalizing,
imprinted on the mind's eye,

the bordered column
carefully filigreed, voluted:
Ionic, Corinthian, classic.

The distant tornado, the furled
mast, the curling corner
of the tear-soaked page,

the fall of the kite from high
in the air, its shimmering color
whorling down around the house,

the flattened grass, your
footprints crossing mine
going the other way
convoluted

# Owls in Daylight

When I wake, I am an old woman,
my flesh a folded living fabric.
I stand in a place I've never been

where I hear in broad daylight
a ceremonious owl there in the woods
where the light falls in lovely lines

across the path, as I gather up
the days and weeks of yesterday,
like small sticks of splintery kindling.

Odd not to feel what I think
as an elder I ought to feel—
frail and helpless, bent into a comma,

a stitch in my stride, my gaze gauzy
and cataracted or just increasingly
myopic from having seen so much:

here, owls in daylight, raccoons
at noon, smart-eyed, parlous,
their delicate black hands prying

everything loose, scratching
through the back screen, as anxious
as I when I've lost my keys.

I know I've lived a lot, my face
mapped and plotted, and what I've seen
I can't unsee: the rose-filled wallpaper

of home, my first room away,
the Deux Chevaux puttering up to Briançon,
the bright white beach at Mykonos,

a lover's hair in salty curls,
the ancient porter in a coastal hotel
north of Belfast, hauling the bags

into the lift, inviting me to squeeze in
beside him, a briefly comic pairing.
The bougainvillea spilling over the wall

on Rhodes, my dead mother's letters
importuning my return, my father wasted
from chemo, his breath as sour

as his words ever were, the old rift
complete now, just another dark image
in the photoplay of my life so long ago,

the bruises faded, the light aslant,
the hour late, but still the owl there,
camouflaged as tree or branch

and thus unseen, yet cadenced, clear,
as present now as at the first, as strong,
and stronger still than love has ever been.

# On *The Book of Kells*

## I. Lapis Lazuli

Precious stones
freighted all the way
from Afghanistan
to Iona, where
they were ground,
stone on stone,
yielding only a tiny
ratio, one to ten,
of the deepest blue,
a breath of heaven
to stroke the bird's wing
curl the lion's tail,
color robe and sandal,
limn the opening
letters of the Book of John,
on vellum for which
two hundred calves
were slaughtered, skinned,
scraped, and buffed
to the glory of the Lord
and for the Great Book,
that unfinished treasure,
held aloft at the sacrifice,
causing jaws to drop
eyes to widen, knees
to bend, before
its stunning pigments,
crowded pages,
mysterious,
forbidding script.

## II. Ink

When the oak wasps
lay their eggs
on the oak branch,
the tree nurtures
them, more carefully
than in the fairy tale
where bountiful trees
speak and hover
to protect the innocent.
The real oak
raises a gall
for the wasp eggs
until they're ready
to bore a hole,
escape and fly away.
But who was it
who first decided
to crush
the oak gall?
Who saw that
the gallic powder
mixed with iron
and bound
with gum Arabic
could be dipped
and applied
to parchment
in angles and curls
lined up close, tighter
than a wasp's nest,
to make meaning?

### III. The Lion

so the story goes,
stood wondering
momentarily
at the stillborn cubs,
as soft and inert
as unleavened bread,
waited three days,
and breathed on them

*spiro    inspiro    spiro*

then: a quickening.

God is the lion,
the dead Son
the cub, and we
the humble scribes
trying to keep
within the lines,
our fanciful mice
chewing on the Host,
just below the feet
of the risen Lord.

## IV. Peacock

Because its flesh
was said not to putrefy,
St. Augustine ordered
a cock cooked,
removed the breast,
saved it for thirty days
and took a look.
Sure enough, fragrance-
free, not food
for worms.
Thus it is
that the bird,
Christ-
like in body
and beauty,
his slender neck
shortened,
his feathers
curtailed,
bends inside
the columns
and corners
of a crowded
page, crouches
inside the arch
over the door
to the next room,
grotesque,
confined.

## V. Vermillion

The alchemists
desiring gold,
as we all do,
cooked mercury
and sulfur
in a fumy
pot that yielded,
not the precious
metal, but smoke
like fire, the
flamiest red
their passion
could imagine.
The Devil
was in this,
they feared.
Never mind,
this hot breath
yielded
a hue redder
than Brazilwood
at its reddest,
brighter
than dragon's
blood,
and hotter.
See how
thoroughly
it bleeds on
the gilded page!

## VI. One Squatting Man Pulling the Beard

of another squatting man
in a silly old quarrel
over beard-beauty
or gold or how
to read a book.
But think what they
could be doing:
gathering armies,
slinging daggers,
or, tied up in knots,
writhing on
the floor, one gripping
the other in a hammer-
lock, spitting and biting,
eyes bulging,
breath laboring
in fits and snorts.
So what if the pulling
stings and hairs
are split, isn't
this better
than the alternative,
doesn't the foolish
face-off
make us smile?

## VII. Gold

On fine parchment
and applied properly,
it does not flake.
Fish glue, made
by grinding
fish eyes and jaws,
helps hold the gold,
as does the Holy Spirit
breathed on the page
by the gilder himself,
exhaling from deep
within onto the gesso,
on a properly humid
day. What served
as barometer,
we ask, how did
the gilder know
when to gild
when to blow,
or, for that matter,
how to hold
the gold,
to keep it
from sliding
away?

# Touch

Caressing the deep sleep marks
on the face of the beloved.
Fingering and marking the page.

Sifting, rinsing, and smiling
at the crowds of small berries
huddled together in the bowl.

The peach at the bottom
of the basket nestled
in its sad death too close

to others not to infect.
So many breathing sneezing
bodies in the metro

trying to stand without
expression or touch, touching
nonetheless, stepping around

and out at the lurch of the stop,
looking down at human feet
shod in human shoes

as they make their way
onto solid ground, up
the stairways, aiming

for the street, striding
forward, laden with bags,
briefcases, wireless connects,

closing in on those ahead
moving faster, trying not
to hear the lone violinist

or make eye contact.
His Brahms eases its way
through the labyrinthine

tunnels, unbuttoning the day,
as coins furtively drop
into the change cup,

an anonymous blessing,
not pressed onto the palm
or placed on the tongue,

but still a gift of hands
gently exposing a wound
or wounds.

# Point of Entry

The rhythmic slapping
of the rope on the ground,
two girls whipping it round
and round:

*Rich man, poor man, beggar man, thief,*
*doctor, lawyer, Indian chief.*

*All in together, girls.*
*How do you like the weather, girls?*

Of course, an eager beginner should run in
exactly on the beat, for she who falters
is lost, ruled Out, shoved aside, maybe
even hit on the head by the rope
or embarrassed to be tangled in it.

Portentous perhaps. A debut of sorts.
Learning when to enter, interrupt, how to
say what and when, to whisper
*The front door's locked, but you can come*
*in the side.* Learning when to change

your vote, raise your hand, when to allow
the lingering ship out of quarantine,
the migrants to cross over the rope
and into the fields. Where—
through hallways, hangars, customs, ports—
to place it, name it: the sentry-less entry,
the boltless door.

# Plato Sounds a Note of Caution

### I.

When the paint slips down the wall
before I can catch it with my brush

I think what Plato said about
the written word: it can double a room,

fill it full or empty it out,
can't be trusted

can't be shrink-wrapped for long,
it'll seep through the plastic

and soil the package, you'll have
blood on your hands at checkout.

You'll have to answer for that
and for your faith in treaty, law.

## II.

Not so long ago women with cancer
of the breast faced their surgery
without anesthesia, a length of rope

in their mouths for grinding and keeping
down the noise, for the sake of the surgeon
and the family, waiting in the parlor below

Yet nowhere to go not to hear
the calling down of curses, propriety
cast aside, as a wrap is thrown on a chair

in abandon, all utterance poisoned,
the silence undressed, violated,
daylight spanked alive

now I am bold to transgress that tale
by catching it on the page
here, holding it fast, still

## III.

The birds don't know!
Sometimes they're named
for the sound of their songs—
*Chuck-will's widow*
*Gotta-find-a-pillow*
*I've seen a gorilla*—
just as easy as that.
Ah yes, Plato feared
the infernal slackness
of words on the page,
their refusal to stand up
straight. They're schoolboys
shooting spitballs
when the master isn't looking.
*See-saw Margery Daw*
*Sold her bed and lay on straw*

Grant's soldiers at Cold Harbor,
sleepless before battle,
wrote their names on scraps
of paper, fingers fumbling,
pinning the names on their jackets
just in case, as though the paper
were stronger than bullets
or blood or earth, as though
no name, no body,
could ever be
entirely lost

# Intercession

Over there
in the middle of nowhere
behold the sun-baked,
crippled toys drowning
in sand, the swing
dangling by one arm
like an amputee.
Behold the tire-less truck
on cement blocks,
a work in progress.
Hull of boat, rust of
trailer, mobile home.

Yet, in spite of it all, honor
the impulse to embellish,
to place bottles in the window,
pretty colors in the sun,
to draw a swirling line
beneath one's signature,
on the lease or the loan,

to fill the space
on the bedroom wall,
a bright poster, Van Gogh,
Renoir, something sweeter
than common talk,
the repetitious expletive,
eternal complaint.

Over the stove,
burners caked in grease,
a sign, a line, a motto,

a reminder of wholeness,
holiness: Do unto
others, say, or two roads
diverged and all that.

Oh, Jesus wept
but not here, not here
where the famished eye
finds solace in yard sale
treasure: flowered glass,
random silver, yellowed
linen, an Eiffel Tower
as small as a thumb,
souvenir postcards,
doilies as complicated
as grandmother's hands.

Hallow the sugar bowl
and matching creamer,
last week's purchase,
both cracked, handles
missing, but imbued
with a sacramental
resilience, a hint of
the eternal quest:
to make it pretty,
make it new,
to make it at all.

Dear God, bless all broken
things, all mended, glued,
bleached and blended,
every tacky stick of it,
every bedside table

tottering on three legs,
every plastic posy
planted by the door
and every gardener who so
would plant. Bless
our small places, the plain
empty spaces, the graceful
blandishment in the mind's eye.

# Substitute

*-for my friend Lois Alworth*

Placing your foot in the circle
without touching the line,
you're a part of the game:

a teacher filling in, an under-
study backstage called forward,
taking the lead, speaking

those words you'd practiced
fervently before the mirror.
You're a part of the play.

You're the pinch hitter, why yes,
moving toward home plate,
swinging that bat, nervous

maybe, yet proud. The one
who comes before, or after,
you're it. Standing next to

the light, all right, but
surely casting its shadow.
The priest came to anoint

the sick man, forgot his
oil. You, the sick man's wife,
ever at his side, retrieved

Canola from your pantry,
the priest prayed over it,
and lo and behold

# Blinders

of ego, place, certitude, circumstance.
As Anna Akhmatova moves in and out
of safety—Ukraine, Paris, Leningrad—
Faulkner moves back to Oxford,
his postage stamp of a world,
taking Sherwood's advice before
joining The Royal Canadians
and acquiring his limp. He will be read
and misunderstood, even excoriated.
The lynchings continue, though rarely
reported, the Klan gathers, and troops
are stretched along many borders.
Africa and the Far East smolder, as
diplomats shuffle among the corridors
of European capitals. Prices climb, fall.
Your mother soaks her lingerie in the sink.
She learns to cook. You are not. Not yet,
but now, perhaps, you are someone's hope.
When Akhmatova's *Requiem* suggests trouble,
her friends commit it to memory so that
it may be neither maligned nor erased.
Though Stalin will surely come after all
of them, he will die before the poet,
whose heart, reamed and scalded, inevitably
gives out. A war ends, another soon begins.
Meanwhile, an early photo: you, in your rompers,
straddle the steel covering the front wheel
of your father's splendid brand-new Buick.
You are, likely, three years old.
The world is your apple.

# Six White Horses

First, let's explore the route,
the rattly mountain road,
the steep pass, the weather.

Let's uncover what word
goes ahead, if any, to herald

that small solitary figure
in the driver's seat.

Let's discover whose practiced
hands grip the reins, whose boots
jam the buckboard,

whose scarf, and of what color,
snaps like a flame of resolve
against the horizon

when the wagon's emptied out
of apples, corn, cast-offs,

or full of pilfered treasure
bending the bone-dry boards,

and why we crowd here by the road
ready to break into song.

If we understand all to come,
those slivers of gold and the cold

wet nights when we'll watch
childhood diminish behind us;

If we, our heads turned only one way,
see her coming round the mountain,

her arrival having nothing to do
with the church nor signifying

a chariot of salvation
nor the ecstasy of orgasm

nothing to do with that,

then we, on tiptoe, facing east,
will see at a distance

her approach, her shouts
startling the air,

and, just above the horses' heads,
our mother's triumphant face.

# About the Author

Sarah Gordon is the author of widely published poems and two previous collections of poetry: *Distances* (Brito & Lair, 1999) and *The Lost Thing* (Mercer University Press, 2022), as well as *Flannery O'Connor: The Obedient Imagination* and *A Literary Guide to Flannery O'Connor's Georgia* (both from the University of Georgia Press, 2000 and 2008, respectively). Professor Emerita at Georgia College & State University in Milledgeville, Gordon chaired five O'Connor symposia at GC and was named Distinguished Professor. She is a recipient of The Governor's Award in the Humanities and now lives in Athens, Georgia.